Encouraging Faith Book

The Just shall live by faith

~ Habakkuk 2:4 ~

by

Imani Williams

1

Unless otherwise indicated, all Scripture quotations are taken from the *New King James Version* of the Bible.

Scripture marked as 'Amplified' are taken from the Amplified Bible. Copyright©1954,1958,1962,1964, 1965,1987 by The Lockman Foundation.

Encouraging Faith Book

ISBN-13: 978-1548477066
ISBN-10: 1548477060

Printed in the United States.
First Printing 2017.

Disclaimer and Terms of Use: No information contained in this book should be considered as legal or medical advice. Your reliance upon information and content obtained by you at or through this publication is solely at your own risk. The author assume no liability or responsibility for damage or injury to you, other persons, or property arising from

An application to register this book for cataloging has been submitted to the Library of Congress.

In memory of my mom

I love you.

Table of Contents

Dear Reader,

Do you know what it really means to be strong? It means not losing your vision, not losing focus, and speaking God's promise when it looks like no hope in sight. It's easy to be strong when things are okay. But can you say "All my needs are met" when you truly need something? Can you say "I am healed" and truly believe it when the doctor diagnosed you with an incurable disease? Can you say "I have more than enough money" when all your bills are due & not enough money to pay them? The good news is: God has already made a way for you! In the Old Testament the Children of Israel and Moses had the Red Sea in front of them and Pharaoh and his soldiers behind them, the Children of Israel panicked & saw no hope.

However, in the midst of that situation Moses said "Fear not! Relax! And see the salvation of the Lord which He will work for you today. For the Egyptians you see today, you will never see them again." It looked like their backs were against the wall and it looked like they were going back into bondage, but in the midst of that Moses believed God would deliver them and God made the impossible happen. It's the devil's mission, and has been since the day in the Garden of Eden, to make us question what God said. More than anything Jesus wants us to believe in him. That's all. Hebrews 10:23 tells us to Keep our focus because God is faithful. I encourage you today with the same words of Moses: "Fear not! Relax! And see the salvation (deliverance) of the Lord which He will work for you today. Don't worry. Have faith. Be strong.

Praying for you always,

Imani

An Issue of the Heart

Proverbs 118:8 - It is better to trust in the Lord than to put confidence in man.

"I don't trust anyone.", "I've been hurt before, I have to protect myself." "I'll never trust again!" Sound familiar? Maybe you feel like this and have said these statements before. If you haven't, you still may have experienced broken trust in a past relationship that has caused you to question whether or not you should trust again. I understand how difficult it can be to trust. Its a known fact that hurt people, hurt people. Though we try our best, no one is perfect. There are times we have been let down by someone or we, even if unintentional, have let someone else down. Trusting is hard. We are human and we err. However, when it comes to God, some of us still have a problem trusting.

Dictionary.com defines trust as reliance on the integrity, strength, ability, and surety of a person or thing; confidence. For example, we trust people who are kind to us and have integrity. We trust someone we can count on to consistently do what's right. Let's look at these scriptures in Proverbs:

Proverbs 3:5-6 - Trust in the Lord with all your heart, and lean not on your own understanding. In all your ways acknowledge Him, and He shall direct your paths.

Based on the definition of trust we know God is consistent, reliable, and have integrity; yet we still have doubts. Let's fix this. Here is where the trust process starts:

Proverbs 3:3 - Let not mercy and truth forsake you; bind them around your neck, write them on the table of your heart.

We know that the truth is the Word of God, and Proverbs is telling us to write this truth on our heart. You write them on your heart with words.

Psalm 45:1 - .... my tongue is the pen of a ready writer.

When you speak & repeat the promises of God over and over you are engraving truth on your heart and it builds your confidence and trust in Him. May I propose to you that trust is more than just deciding to believe something or someone. Trust is a continuous action that sets you on a path of consistent victory. I want to take a moment to look at David's prayer in Psalm 16:

Psalm 16:1 - Preserve me, O God, for in You I put

my trust.

Here is something important: In the title of Psalm 16 it says that this Psalm is a Michtam of David. Michtam in Hebrew means engraving. Engraving means to carve on the surface of something hard. Past experiences that are bad can surely make our hearts hard, but our diligence in prayer, worship, and speaking the Word of God over our situations is part of the engraving process of our hearts and it helps in building trust.

Psalm 16:7-10 - I will bless the Lord who has given me counsel; my heart also instructs me in the night seasons. I have set the Lord always before me; Because He is at my right hand I shall not be moved. Therefore my heart is glad, and my glory rejoices; My flesh also will rest in hope. For you will not leave my soul in Sheol, nor will You allow your saintly one to see corruption.

In verse 10 the word corruption in Hebrew is Shachath which means "a pit" as in a trap. Reading and meditating on the Word of God and listening to God is important. David was always after God's heart. He was always in the presence of God engraving promises on his heart. So much so that during the trials of life or the "dark seasons" the

11

things in his heart instructed, guided, encouraged, and gave him hope. David had confidence in God.

When you trust God, you will allow Him to lead you in the dark moments and you will bypass traps and snares. When you find yourself struggling to decide whether or not to trust God, it's important to figure out why. Has He let me down in some way? Has He lead me astray? If you will be honest, your answers will be No. He hasn't. David finishes his prayer by saying:

Psalm 16:11-You will show me the path of life; In Your presence is fullness of joy; at Your right hand are pleasures for ever more.

Trusting God is more than just saying "I'm going to trust God." Its the action of constantly reminding yourself of why you trust Him. When you do this you will remember the times when He came through for you before. Surely He can do it again! Jesus said in John 10:10 that He comes into our lives to bring us a God kind of life and he wants us to enjoy life to its fullest. He will never leave you nor forsake you and he will help you. You will see that he will not leave you in a mess. He will not leave you in confusion. Choose to trust him at all times in every circumstance. He created you, He knows you. He loves you.

Pause and think on that!

Psalm 3:5 - Then I lay down and slept in peace and woke up safely, for the Lord was watching over me.

David wrote this psalm while fleeing from his son, Absalom. It reveals the battle that went on inside him as he lived in fear. He says:

Psalm 3:1-2 - O Lord, so many are against me. So many seek to harm me. I have so many enemies. 2 So many say that God will never help me. Selah

You know when you're going through something and it feels like that problem/person/situation that is troubling you is getting worse and worse? You're overwhelmed and full of fear because you don't know what is going to happen next. This is what David was feeling at the time he wrote this psalm. For most of us, it is our initial reaction to feel fear and complain when the heat is turned up in our lives. David continues to say:

Psalm 3:3-8 - I cried out to the Lord, and he heard me (from his Temple in Jerusalem.)" Selah 5 Then I lay down and slept in peace and woke up safely, for the Lord was watching over me. 6 And now, although ten thousand enemies surround me on every side, I am not afraid. 7 I will cry to him, "Arise, O Lord! Save me, O my God!" And he will slap them in the face, insulting them and breaking

off their teeth." 8 For salvation comes from God.
What joys he gives to all his people. Selah"

Notice at the end of some statements David puts the word "Selah". The Amplified Bible translates selah as "pause, and think of that." The quality I like most about David is even though he is feeling fearful and is complaining about his current circumstances, he immediately strengthens himself by turning to the Lord and remembering that the Lord is there for him, watching over him, and will help him. He does this several times in the Psalms. One moment David is worried and complaining. Next moment David is full of faith. Was David double-minded? No. We all are human. We feel fear when negative things happen to us, but remember this promise:

Psalm 55:22 - Cast your cares on the LORD and he will sustain you; he will never let the righteous be shaken.

We should immediately snap back to the truth of God's promises to us. No matter what you are going through, Don't focus on the problem, turn to God. Meditate (selah) on His promises, like Psalm 55:22. He will not allow you to be shaken. He cares for you. He loves you. Can you be like David and find peace in trusting in the Lord? Turn all your fears over to Him. Do not be afraid of the unknown. It may be unknown to you, but God knows all. Trust Him. Selah!

(pause, and think on that)

Pour out your heart, He hears

Psalms 34:15 - The eyes of the Lord are on the righteous and his ears are open to their cry.

In the training class I'm teaching at this time, I teach people how to become effective Christian counselors. One of the effective principles, and a very important skill I teach is empathetic listening. Empathetic listening is being able to hear with your eyes, your ears, and your heart. It's being so in-tune with the speaker that you hear what they are saying and what they are not saying.

Here in Psalms 34:15 we see that our Lord listens empathetically. His eyes are looking at your body language, facial expressions, and seeing your tears. His ears hear your tone of voice, your cries and he feels your pain. It sometimes seem that when one bad circumstance let up, here comes another. It's enough to make you cry aloud. With smartphones, the Internet, and so many other distractions it seems as if no one has the time or even care to listen when you're hurting. However, there is One who is waiting by with open ears, open eyes, and an open heart to hear everything you have to say and open arms to embrace you in the midst of the trying time to let you know He's there, He sees, He hears, and He Loves You.

Psalms 34:18 says he is near those with a broken heart and saves those with a broken spirit. Close your eyes and imagine Him right there, right now, right next to you with His loving arms around you listening, seeing, and telling you "Everything will be alright." While you are crying and pouring out your heart, The Lord hears you and He will deliver you. He can do something about your situation (see Psalms 34:17-20). He will help you and get you out of your problem Unscathed. Read Psalms 34. Let it minister to your heart. He hears and He helps. He is the Wonderful Counselor.

Trip down Memory lane

"Psalms 124:1 –"If it had not been the Lord who was on our side"

In this psalm you see David is taking a trip down memory lane and remembering all the battles that resulted in victories and is confessing his total dependence on the Lord. He is letting the world know:

"If it had not been the Lord who was on our side,"

Let Israel now say--

2 "If it had not been the Lord who was on our side,

When men rose up against us,

3 Then they would have swallowed us alive, when their wrath was kindled against us;

4 Then the waters would have overwhelmed us,

The stream would have gone over our soul;

5 Then the swollen waters would have gone over our soul."

6 Blessed be the Lord, who has not given us as prey to their teeth.

7 Our soul has escaped as a bird from the snare of

the fowlers (bird hunters);

The snare is broken, and we have escaped.

8 Our help is in the name of the Lord,

Who made heaven and earth.

Notice David is recounting the details, one a little worse than the one before it. How many times have we been in situations and with each moment it gets worse and worse? Let us take a moment to take a trip down memory lane: Think about that situation or situations that were too overwhelming for you to handle. Bills due, no money. The car needs to be fixed. Husband not acting right. Wife not acting right. Kids not acting right. The people at work have totally lost their minds. Think about the waters, the tears you've cried, the sleepless nights. Think about the traps that had been laid for you to get caught in….. BUT GOD!!!!

As David says in verse 6: Blessed be the Lord who didn't let you fall prey to any of this. Think about the traps you got caught in and the Lord broke them in order for you to escape. Verse 8 says: "our help is in the Name of the Lord who made heaven and earth" Tell me, who can defeat the one who made all things, know all things, and can do all things? This is the One who is on your side to help you out of any situation and circumstance. There is NOTHING TOO HARD FOR GOD. Think about this: If it had not been for the Lord on my side, where would I be? I am totally dependent on the Lord to get me through the day, the next hour, the next minute, and the next second. It is because of him we live, and move, and breathe. It is because of Him we are more than conquerors. It is because of him that our feet are like hinds feet and we can leap over the mountains of trouble. You know what; I feel like David, it's time for a praise break. Celebrate Him Right Now.

Never Alone

Matthew 14:30 - But when he saw that the wind was boisterous, he was afraid; and beginning to sink he cried out, saying, "Lord, save me!"

Here in Matthew 14, Jesus made his disciples get into a boat and go to the other side while he, Jesus, sent the multitudes away and took some alone time to pray. Now, while the disciples are sailing in the middle of the sea, a very strong wind comes and waves are tossing the boat around. Have you ever found yourself in a situation and wondered "Lord, how did I get here?"...

You're being tossed back and forth. You've been tossed around so much, you don't even know which end is up anymore. Sometimes we find ourselves in situations where we don't know how we got there and we don't know how to get out. But right in the middle of the wind and the waves, right in the middle of the mess that's taking place in your life, here comes Jesus walking on the water. While you are crying out in fear, He's saying "Have hope, It's me, don't be afraid" Peter says, "Lord, if its really you, tell me to come to you on the water" Jesus says "Come." Miraculously, Peter begins to walk on the water. Then when he looks around and see the tall waves being blown by the strong winds, he begins to doubt if he can continue walking and starts to sink.

How many times have we found ourselves in situations where the winds are strong, the waves are high and we feel we can't make it. We say "Lord, I can't do this! I'm scared!" We feel like we're sinking in this mess and there is no hope. Think about this: the whole time while Peter was having this battle with fear in his mind and sinking, Jesus, the one who told him to come out in the first place, was right there. Peter, overwhelmed with fear, screams "LORD, SAVE ME!!!" Immediately, Jesus stretched out his hand and caught him and they walked back to the boat together. Can you see Jesus having this pep talk with Peter on the way back to the boat while walking on the water saying "You know Peter, if I didn't think you could do it, I wouldn't have told you to do it. O, you of little faith. Why did you doubt? I was right there with you."

One of the names of God from the book of Ezekiel 48:35 is Jehovah Shammah meaning The Lord is there. He is there, right there with you today and He will be there with you always. Psalms 46:1 says that God is our refuge and our strength, a very present help in trouble. Just like with Peter, Jesus is standing there telling you to come. "Come out of that situation you are in. Step out of the boat. You can do it. I know the waters are rough and the wind is strong and everything around you looks like chaos, but I wouldn't tell you to come out if I didn't know you would be safe." And at that moment when you begin to doubt yourself and you feel yourself sinking, He is standing right there with an out-stretched hand waiting to catch you. In Matthew 28:20 Jesus says "Lo, I am with you always, even unto the end of the world." No matter what you are going through always remember, you are never alone. The One who confidently walks on the waters of trouble is with you to help you do the same.

True Love

John 3:16 - For God so loved the world that He gave His only begotten Son, that whoever believes in Him should not perish but have everlasting life.

We all fall. We all make mistakes. We all sin. God knew we would mess up and he made a way for us to be right and not lose fellowship with him. Many people feel that they must do something to gain favor with God. "If I just pray 3 times a day", "If I read my bible 10 times a day" etc... "then God will not be mad with me". All these thing are great things to do, and they surely benefit us in our walk with God, but honestly..nothing we do makes us righteous. Works (the things we do to try to impress God) do not make us righteous. Only Jesus Christ and what he did for us and our faith (believing what he did for us) makes us right. Christ is our savior. The once and for all sacrifice. We can't save ourselves. We need a savior. Every day we need saving from something. We are not perfect. But through Jesus we are made perfect because when God sees you , he sees Jesus in you. *(see 1 John 4:10-17).*

When we mess up we must repent. Repent doesn't just mean to say "I'm sorry" it means to turn away from your old way of doing things. Psalm 119:59

says "I have considered my ways (of doing things) and have turned my steps to your way" Don't be deceived. Christ did not die to declare us right so we can keep sinning. (see Romans 6:1). Sin makes life hard on us and hard for us. Sin keeps us from living the life God intended for us. Christ died that we might enjoy life, a more abundant life, overflowing with his blessings.(see John 10:10). Sin and condemnation keeps us from experiencing this kind of life. Jesus does not condemn us, the devil does. He knows that if he can convince us that we are not worthy of God's love or God's promises, we reject what Jesus did on the cross for us. Do not let this happen.

Romans 8:1 says: There is therefore now no condemnation to those who are in Christ Jesus. Hebrews 10:23 - Let us hold fast or hold on tightly to our profession (confession) of faith (what we believe) without wavering. Here is what we believe: God loves us so much He sent himself in His son who gave His life for the world that through him we are saved, redeemed and righteous and have eternal life. Think about this: Every evening God would walk with Adam and Eve through the Garden of Eden. I imagine they walked, talked, laughed and had a great time together. When Adam and Eve sinned in the Garden of Eden, they let guilt and condemnation set in and they became ashamed and ran away from God. God, all knowing, knew what they had done, yet he still came to their special meeting place so they could have their evening walk together. God's love for us is unfathomable. You can't understand it, just receive it.

When you sin don't run from him, run to him. This is the reason Christ came to the world in the first place. To illustrate: I have two children and we all know that kids mess up. Hey, they're kids, they are still learning. When they disobey me, does that stop me from loving them? No, of course not! I love them regardless of what they do. In the same way, we are God's children and we are still learning. When we mess up, no matter how, he still loves us. Find freedom in knowing that God's love for you Never fails.

A Done Deal

Hebrews 8:6-12 -

But now He has obtained a more excellent ministry, inasmuch as He is also Mediator of a better covenant, which was established on better promises. A New Covenant 7 For if that first covenant had been faultless, then no place would have been sought for a second. 8 Because finding fault with them, He says: "Behold, the days are coming, says the Lord, when I will make a new covenant with the house of Israel and with the house of Judah-- 9 not according to the covenant that I made with their fathers in the day when I took them by the hand to lead them out of the land of Egypt; because they did not continue in My covenant, and I disregarded them, says the Lord. 10 For this is the covenant that I will make with the house of Israel after those days, says the Lord: I will put My laws in their mind and write them on their hearts; and I will be their God, and they shall be My people. 11 None of them shall teach his neighbor, and none his brother, saying, 'Know the Lord,' for all shall know Me, from the least of them to the greatest of them. 12 For I will be merciful to their unrighteousness, and their sins and their lawless deeds I will remember no more." 13 In that He says, "A new covenant," He has made the first obsolete. Now what is becoming obsolete and growing old is ready to vanish away.

This is the Great News of the gospel people!!! Under the old covenant we had to do ALL of the law then God would bless us. However, He knew we wouldn't be able to. Since we couldn't keep every commandment of the law & he didn't want to keep us bound to something impossible for us to do (for his yoke is easy & his burden is light) he gave a new covenant through his son Jesus. Jesus, the once and for all sacrifice for all our sin. All we have to do is believe. Believe that God is merciful and has forgiven our sins and He remembers them no more. Believe he is our God. Believe Jesus paid a debt that was rightfully ours.

Some think that if people knew that God is merciful and remembers sin no more, it will give them a license to sin. Absolutely not! Think about this: God sent himself in His Son and He died not only FOR you; but He died AS you. He chose to take the punishment we rightfully deserve upon himself because He loves us. Why would one continue to sin? I will do whatever he says. I choose to live right because I want to, not because I'm obligated to. Even when we do sin, Romans 5:20

says that grace much more abound and we just have to believe that. Believing is our part of the new contract through Jesus Christ. Believing that because of Jesus' once and for all sacrifice on the cross we have total access to our heavenly Father and have everything we need. All we have to do is believe that God is God, that he is whatever we need, believe everything he says in the New covenant/testament, and he will do the blessing.

Notice in the Old Covenant, The Ten Commandments, God says "You shall not....., you shall not....., etc...." but in the New Covenant in verses 10 through 12 God is saying "I will...., I will..., I will. Remember in the Old Covenant we had to do something then God would do something in return. Even today we sometimes feel we have to do something to earn Gods grace. We do not. Jesus already did for us the thing we had to do. When he said it is finished on the cross that meant he did it. He did it all. Thank you, Jesus! We want healing... We don't have to earn it, All we have to do is believe that God is our God and he is merciful and he Is A Healer. Everything is about believing. God told Moses "I am that I am." That means:

I am (whatever you need)

(what you need) that I am

With this New Contract that we have through Jesus Christ you have everything you will ever need. What is it that you need today? Healing, peace of mind, a financial blessing..... whatever it is, it is covered in the contract. Just believe it's a done deal!

Random Declaration:

"I will trust God no matter what is going on in my life right now. God knows what's best for me, and I trust Him. Thank you, Lord for getting me through this"

Speak life to that dead situation

Ezekiel 37: 1-3 - The hand of the Lord came upon me and brought me out in the Spirit of the Lord, and set me down in the midst of the valley; and it was full of bones....And He said to me, "Son of man, can these bones live?"...

Here Ezekiel has been taken by The Lord to a valley that was full of dry human bones. Everywhere he looked everything was dead, dry, showing no signs of life at all. Have you found yourself in dry situations before? Are you in a lifeless situation right now and feel there is no hope? I've surely found myself in these types of situations many times. Yes, it seems hopeless and so do I. I imagine this is how Ezekiel must have felt looking around this valley at the many dry human bones laying around. Death was all around him. Then The Lord asks him "Son of Man can these bones live?" This is a really weird question, right? Bones, coming to life again? Why would God ask this question, it seems impossible?! Well, people, this is a great illustration showing that what we see and what God sees are totally different. What we may see as a hopeless, dry & dead situation, God sees it as an opportunity to show his excellent power in our lives.

"Son of Man can these bones live?" Ezekiel, being such a smart guy, did not say no, and he didn't say yes either. Sometimes we don't have the answers to our situation but because we don't have the answers, it is not wise to speak negatively or complain about it. Ezekiel left it open for God to work by saying "Lord, you know!" Instead of complaining about what's happening around us or to us or talking about the negativity, it is wise to leave it in the hands of The Lord and say "Lord, you know." When Ezekiel left the situation in God's hands, The Lord gave him the answer. Notice what happened next:

" Again He said to me, "Prophesy to these bones, and say to them, 'O dry bones, hear the word of the Lord! Thus says the Lord God to these bones: "Surely I will cause breath to enter into you, and you shall live. I will put sinews on you and bring flesh upon you, cover you with skin and put breath in you; and you shall live. Then you shall know that I am the Lord." Ezekiel 37:4-6

Wait, wait, wait,.... Is God saying that all we have to do is speak to dead things and they will live? Yes! That is exactly what He is saying. Notice the faith of Ezekiel:

"So I prophesied as I was commanded; and as I

prophesied, there was a noise, and suddenly a
rattling; and the bones came together, bone to
bone. Indeed, as I looked, the sinews and the flesh
came upon them, and the skin covered them over;
but there was no breath in them." - Ezekiel 37:7-8

Ezekiel obeyed what God told him and spoke to
the bones! I'm sure he felt silly talking to bones, but
as he spoke, there was a noise and a rattling, and the
bones came together. It may seem silly speaking into
the atmosphere, saying something that you don't see
in reality. Yes, the fact may be that you do not have a
job and no money right now, but the truth is God
supplies all of your needs. (Phil 4:19) The truth is
God gives you the power to get wealth
(Deuteronomy 8:18) Remember God's truth overrule
the facts. I'm telling you that when you stand in
confidence and speak God's Word to the seemingly
hopeless, dead situations in your life, all of a sudden
you will see things start to come together. The
impossible starts to happen.

Verses 9 & 10: Also He said to me, "Prophesy to
the breath, prophesy, son of man, and say to the
breath, 'Thus says the Lord God: "Come from the
four winds, O breath, and breathe on these slain, that
they may live." So I prophesied as He commanded
me, and breath came into them, and they lived, and
stood upon their feet, an exceedingly great army.

So here it is, In obedience to God, Ezekiel spoke to the dead, dry bones, and bones came together, muscles formed, skin formed, and breath came into the bones and they lived and stood on their feet and it was like looking at a great army.

God wants to give life to the "dead" things in our lives. Can anything great come from a past of failure? Can healing come to someone who has been ill for most of their life? Can a hopeless situation in your marriage, with your children, with your career/job/business change? Absolutely! I'm not saying that change happens overnight, although it could, but being obedient by constantly speaking the promises of God over your life and having confidence in God knowing that He is there for you, will provide for you, and want to see you live your best life right now; you will notice things will begin to line up in your favor. Have faith and Don't give up when things seem hopeless. Speak Life to those dead things and watch God's power show up!

If he did it before...

1 Samuel 17:37 - Moreover David said, "The Lord, who delivered me from the paw of the lion, and from the paw of the bear, He will deliver me from the hand of this Philistine."

This is one of my favorite events in history. In 1 Samuel 17, the Philistine army and the Israelite army are preparing for battle at Sochoh. The Philistines stood on a mountain on one side, and Israel stood on a mountain on the other side, with a valley between them. Everyday and every night for forty days this champion warrior named Goliath would come down to the valley and taunt Israel. Goliath was very intimidating. He was nine feet tall, wore heavy armor from head to toe, had heavy weapons and a heavy shield. Not only that, he would "trash-talk" to put fear in the hearts of the Israelite army and it worked.

Goliath was so confident in himself that he decided to be the representative for the whole Philistine army. He says "Choose a man for yourselves, and let him come down to fight me..." What began as a battle of armies became a one-on-one fight between two men. The loser and the army he represented would become the servants of the winner. This was too much for Israel, they were scared of this guy. The Bible says Israel was dismayed and greatly afraid.

Have you ever been in a place where this "giant" of a situation has presented itself to you and has put fear in your heart? You're scared of it. You can't sleep at night because you're worried about it. You look around for help in your "army" of friends and family and NO ONE will help you. Every moment you are awake, this giant keeps taunting you: "Your bill is due soon, and you don't have the money to pay it!", ""You are worthless, hopeless, and nobody cares about you, not even your own family", "How are you even going to make it this week?", "Your grandparents marriage failed, your parents marriage failed, your friend, who just got married, marriage is failing. There is no hope for you either, just give up!", "You are in debt up to your eyeballs, don't even think about getting out of it! You have no skills, you're under employed, you can't afford to go back to school, just give up on that idea." The "Goliath" just won't let up. What is one to do when situations like this arise? Let's find out:

In verses 12-29 A young guy named David is on his way to Israel's camp to bring his brothers, who were part of the army, lunch. When he gets there he sees this huge warrior taunting the army and the effect it is having on Israel. David gets offended! (paraphrasing) "How dare this Philistine defy the armies of the living God, who does he think he is!!" Then one of David's brothers get mad with him and says " Why are you even here?! Who is tending the sheep? Go do what you always do, David!" Notice what is happening here. The army of Israel is being intimidated by Goliath, and when David shows a little bit of boldness, his brother comes up to intimidate him. Isn't that just how it goes? When you start to show a little courage to change your situation, someone comes up to transfer their negative emotions on you? They come with negative comments to discourage you. David did not let the intimidation of the Philistine warrior or his brother get to him. David says in verse 32: "Let no man's heart fail because of him, I will go and fight with this Philistine."

What!!!????? David, a shepherd and musician with no warrior experience has agreed to boldly go and fight this giant. How can he do this? What gives David the guts to go fight someone who is bigger and stronger than him? This is how: pay attention this next statement made by David:

1 Samuel 17:34-37: Your servant (meaning himself) used to keep his father's sheep, and when a lion or bear came and took a lamb of the flock, I

*went out after it and struck it and delivered the
lamb from it's mouth; and when it arose against
me, I caught it by it's beard, and struck and killed it
(with his bare hands). I've killed both the lion and
the bear; and this uncircumcised Philistine will be
like one of them, seeing as he defied the armies of
the living God. The Lord who delivered me from
the paw of the lion and the bear, He will deliver me
from the hand of this Philistine."*

In other words David said: God has delivered me
before, he is surely able to deliver me again. To make
a long story short, David goes into the valley with
the only thing he had: His sling shot, 5 smooth
stones, and his confidence in God. David declared
his faith out loud in front of everyone and the Lord
delivered him and the army of Israel that day. He
killed Goliath with a rock. Did you know that you
have inside of you this same faith and courage that
David had this day? Did you also know that you have
a rock to slay that Goliath in your life? That Rock
you have is Jesus. Have confidence today that the
Lord that has delivered you many times before is
surely able to deliver you from whatever giant you
are facing today. When you put your confidence
God, the impossible happens in your life.

God so desperately wants us to totally trust,
depend, and rely on Him. In the New Testament

Jesus tells us in Mark 9:23: Only believe. All things are possible to him that believes. God is faithful. He will never let you down. Stand boldly in the face of that situation and be like David and put your confidence in God and find peace in knowing that if he delivered you before, He will surely deliver you again.

Have confidence in God

Numbers 13:30 – Then Caleb quieted the people before Moses, and said, "Let us go up at once and take possession, for we are well able to overcome it."

In the last post I talked about David and his encounter with a giant. Since we are on the subject of giants, I'm reminded of another event in history with giants. Allow me to tell you the story. It's pretty long, but there is an important message in it.

Moses and the Israelites have made their exodus out of Egypt and now are in the wilderness of Paran. The Lord tells Moses send one leader from each of the twelve tribes to survey the land which he promised to give them, the land that flowed with milk and honey. So Moses chose the leaders, gave them the directions and told them to survey the land then come back and report what it was like. The spies go over there to check out the land and literally everything is awesome. How awesome? They brought back a cluster of grapes that were so big that two men had to carry it between them on a pole. This was the report from the surveyors (spies):

Numbers 13:27-29: "We went to the land where you sent us. It truly flows with milk and honey, and this is its fruit. Nevertheless the people who dwell in the land are strong; the cities are fortified and very large; moreover we saw the descendants of Anak there. (The descendants of Anak are the nephilim, or the giants. These people were between 15 and 40 feet tall. That's why the grapes were so big) The Amalekites dwell in the land of the south, the Hittites, Jebusites, and the Amorites dwell in the mountains, and the Canaanites dwell by the sea and along the banks of Jordan."

The Lord was letting them have a peek at what was coming in their future. One person got excited about this, his name was Caleb. Caleb was so excited that he said: (verse 30) "Let us go up AT ONCE and take possession, for we are well able to overcome it." Caleb was ready! The others around him said: "We are not able to go up against these people, for they are stronger than we. There are giants over there! We were like grasshoppers in OUR OWN SIGHT, and so were we in their sight"

Isn't it something how when you get a peek at what God has for you and get excited about it, someone who has no victory in their life comes along and tries to discourage you and tell you how you aren't qualified to have victory either. Caleb saw the same things that the others saw, yet Caleb had something the others lacked: faith in God and vision. Caleb envisioned himself walking around this amazing place, living in one of the beautiful homes, laying back chowing down on a grape the size of a basketball …(Remember they are coming from a place where they were enslaved so I think his imagination probably ran wild.) Caleb knew that if God promised them this land, he would make a way for them to get it. Caleb saw a land of giants and envisioned Israel taking over and possessing that land.

The others saw the land of giants and envisioned themselves as small, weak, and incompetent. Then they said: "Oh, if only we had died in Egypt, or died in the wilderness. Why would God lead us here to this place to die by the sword in this land and let our wives and children become victims?" Then they started looking for someone to take them back to Egypt. Now, remember what God did for them prior to this point: He delivered them from slavery in Egypt, parted the Red Sea for them to walk on dry ground, gave them fresh manna every morning to eat when they complained of being hungry, when they complained about being tired of eating manna, he gave them quail, He gave them water when they got thirsty, He gave them shade during the daytime hours so they wouldn't be hot, and gave them fire at night so they wouldn't be cold. For some reason, they thought God had brought them this far to let them die by the hand of these giants. Joshua, another one of the spies and a visionary full of faith like Caleb, even tried to talk some sense into them: "If God brought us here, he will surely give us the land…Do not fear them!" (Numbers 14:6-9). After all the things God had brought them through…… Even God had to point that out:

Numbers 14:11 – Then the Lord said to Moses: "How long will these people reject Me? And how long will they not believe Me, with all the signs I've performed among them?" (Then God got mad) "I will strike them with pestilence and disinherit them…."

Well, Moses talked to God and pleaded for mercy on their behalf and God didn't strike them down. However, those who had no faith and complained against God did not get to go to the Promised Land. You know who did get to go: Caleb, Joshua, and the children of the people who complained. In verse 11, you see right there that God really wants us to trust, rely, believe, and depend on him. Complaining shows your lack of faith and trust in God.

Why is it so easy to forget God's goodness when we feel threatened, tired, disappointed, or dissatisfied? We complain as if God isn't there with us to help us. Learn a lesson from the Israelites: when you feel tempted to complain, DON'T. Many times the situations we find ourselves in are beyond our ability to handle them, but complaining about it doesn't help.   Remember this: NOTHING IS BEYOND GOD'S CAPABILITES. Don't look at how "giant" your circumstance is, realize how much bigger your God is. No "giant" can stand in the way of what God promised you. Later on in the book of Joshua, Caleb drove out three giants that were on his "promised land." Nothing is too hard for God. Take a moment and think about all that God has brought you through. God wants to bring you to a new place. He wants to do something new for you, and through you. Think about that dream that God has put on the inside of you. Think about that invention, that book, or that million dollar idea God gave you. It may seem impossible to possess, but don't be intimidated by it and complain, and back away from it. Heed the words of Caleb and Joshua: "Go up at once and take possession, for you are well able to overcome it. If God brought you to it, he will surely give it to you" Take courage, have faith in God and go possess it.

Keep Calm & Have confidence in God

Mark 4:40 - But He said to them, "Why are you so fearful? How is it that you have no faith?"

On this day Jesus left the house to sit by the sea. While he's sitting there teaching, people start gathering around him to the point that a large multitude forms and there is no more room on the shore for him to sit. So Jesus gets into a boat, sits, and teaches from there while the crowd stays on the shore. When he was done teaching for the day, His disciples got into the boat where He was and Jesus tells them: "Let's go to the other side." Now, they've left the multitudes and are now sailing on the sea. While they are sailing, a great windstorm arose. Waves are beating into the boat, water is beginning to fill the boat and the disciples are scared and in fear of death. While all this is happening, Jesus is in the back part of the boat sleeping. How? (and most importantly) Why? Well, the disciples had that same question. Mark 4:38 says: They awoke him and said to him: "Teacher, do You not care that we are perishing?" Doesn't this sound like us sometimes? "Lord, do you not see what I am going through here?! Don't you care about what's happening to me right now?!" Of course he does! However, notice what Jesus does, and this is the point of this message: verse 39-40:

Then He arose and rebuked the wind, and said to the sea, "Peace, be still!" And the wind ceased and there was a great calm. But he said to them: "Why are you so fearful? How is it that you have no faith?"

Even though Jesus said prior to embarking: "Let us go to the other side," the disciples did not believe they were going to make it because of this storm. Jesus had total confidence that they all would make it to the other side. That is why he was able to sleep through such a terrifying experience.

Do you have enough faith to rest in the midst of the storm happening in your life right now? Do you totally trust that Jesus is with you and will not let the storm consume you? Allow me to rephrase Jesus' words in verse 40 like this: "Why are you full of fear and not full of faith?" Jesus has given us so many promises that cover every single area of our lives, yet we aren't using our faith to see them come to pass. I believe that Jesus at the greatest wanted to see his disciples do what he did which was speak to that storm so it would calm down, and at the very least he

46

did not want to see them be fearful and panic while the storm was happening. He wants us to trust in him and trust in his word.

Panicking showed Jesus that they had no faith, and if they did have it, they weren't using it. So how do we show we have faith? Two ways: #1. By speaking to the storms of life and #2 at the least not panicking when the storm comes and placing total confidence in God to bring us through it. Whatever storm you are going through today, The Lord gave you a promise of victory. Maybe it isn't "Let's go to the other side." Maybe for you its': "By His stripes, you are healed". Maybe it's: "No weapon formed against you shall prosper, and every word that comes up to judge you will be shown to be in the wrong." Whatever it is, have enough confidence in God and his Word for your situation and stick with it, hold on to it. Don't panic when the wind picks up and the waves are hitting the boat and the water is starting to fill the boat because Hebrews 10:23 tells us "Let us hold fast the profession of our faith without wavering; (for he is faithful that promised;)

When life gives you lemons... Don't make lemonade

1 Samuel 30:8 So David inquired of the Lord, saying "Shall I pursue this troop? Shall I over take them?" And He answered him, "Pursue, for you shall surely overtake them and without fail recover all."

You know that saying "When life gives you lemons, make lemonade". This is a phrase used to encourage optimism in the face of adversity . "Lemons" refer to an unfortunate or inadequate situation. "Lemonade" on the other hand, is a sweetened form of this same fruit, and so in the context of this expression, conveys the potential for pleasure and opportunity in seemingly bad situations. Turning lemons into lemonade is great, but to be honest, I'm tired of making lemonade; and I am sick and tired of the one who is passing out the lemons. The Bible says:

"The thief does not come except to steal, and to kill, and to destroy. ..." – John 10:10a

The thief, the devil, our enemy is the one passing out the lemons. He can't stand for us to have peace so he throws "lemons" into our lives. He doesn't like for us to be healthy and strong so he throws a "lemon" called sickness or disease to try to make us unhealthy. He hates for us to have peace of mind so he throws a "lemon" grenade to make all types of negative thoughts come to our minds. He tries everything in his arsenal to make us feel defeated. His mission has been to rob us of everything good.

In 1 Samuel 30:1-6 David and his men have returned from a military mission to find that their enemy had attacked their camp, burned it with fire and had taken captive the women and children. They did not kill anyone, but carried them away. The men that were with David are distressed and are crying aloud and weeping. Sadness then turns to bitterness and they are ready to stone David for having them go on that mission with him. After all, if they had been home, maybe they could have protected their families. When the devil wreak havoc in our lives, we get distressed, we feel down, we feel sorry for ourselves, and we want to blame someone else, but this is the wrong response. Notice what David does:

1 Samuel 30:6b – But David strengthened himself in the Lord his God.

49

This is what we must do in times of distress. Do not cower. We must strengthen ourselves in the Lord. Be strong. Whatever you do to strengthen yourself in the Lord, do it. Sing, declare in faith what you want to see, read his promises from the bible, whatever it is, do it. Then, consult with God in prayer.

1 Samuel 30:7-8: Then David said to Abiathar the priest, Ahimelech's son, "Please bring the ephod here to me." And Abiathar brought the ephod to David. So David inquired of the Lord, saying, "Shall I pursue this troop? Shall I overtake them?"

Notice his prayer: David didn't pray: "Oh, Lord, what am I going to do? This is terrible! Woe is me!" David asked "Shall I pursue this troop? Shall I overtake them?" He wasn't asking "Shall I" as a question of his ability to do it, but "Shall I" as in permission to go do it. David prayed as a victor, one who could pursue his enemy and defeat them. God's response is: (verse 8) "Pursue, for you shall surely overtake them and without fail recover all." All that the enemy has stolen, you have the right and authority to recover it!

So, back to the quote about lemons… (I am

rephrasing a quote from Cave Johnson of the video game Portal 2 and I'm going to replace the word "life" with the words "the devil")

"When the devil gives you lemons, don't make lemonade. Make the devil take the lemons back! Get mad! I don't want your lemons, what am I supposed to do with these? Make the devil rue the day he thought he could give [insert your name here] lemons! Do you know who I am!"

You are not a victim but a Victor! Take a stand today and say: **ENOUGH IS ENOUGH!** No longer allow the enemy to come into your life, home, family, relationship, job, etc. and rob you of the peace, happiness, joy, love, good health, the dream, etc.. that rightfully belongs to you. And for what he has stolen, don't let him get away with what he has done. Pursue, and you shall overtake him, and without fail Recover all!

Keys that unlock the door to peace

Philippians 4:7 – and the peace of God, which surpasses all understanding, will guard your hearts and minds through Christ Jesus.

All of us are going through something, and peace is just what we need during these trying times. Here in the book of Philippians, Paul is giving us the keys to having the peace of God in our lives. The first key is he tells us to Rejoice!

Philippians 4:4 – Rejoice in the Lord always. Again, I will say rejoice.

What does this mean to "rejoice in the Lord?" Well, let's look at the word rejoice. Rejoice means to be glad; take delight (followed by in). If we break the word down more we can see it like this: Re- means "again" or "again and again". Joy is a feeling of great pleasure and happiness or delight. So, rejoice means to delight again and again. In this verse, Paul is not asking us but is commanding us to delight again and again in the Lord. This lets us know it is our responsibility to feel this way. We are to purposely have joy. The attitude of rejoicing is something that we control. Joy is independent of our circumstances. We can choose to have joy in the midst of a trial!

The second key is to remain calm.

Philippians 4:5 - Let your gentleness be known to all men. The Lord is at hand.

As I have said in previous posts, how we respond to the not so pleasant circumstances in our lives shows where our level of trust in God is. We should be known as people who do not "sweat." (Remember my post "Keep Calm and Have Faith" where Jesus was in the back of the boat sleeping while a terrible storm was going on?) We as Christians should always remain calm no matter what is happening around us. How is it that we can remain cool when the "heat" has been turned up in our situation? Well, because the Lord is at hand. "At hand" means near by. Being calm should be like second nature to us because God is at our side. If you truly believe that God is near by, then there is no need to worry.

The third key is to pray & be thankful instead of worrying.

Philippians 4:6 - Be anxious for nothing, but in everything by prayer and supplication, with thanksgiving, let your requests be made known to God.

Worrying is never good. Look at some of the effects worrying has on a person's body:

Headache

Muscle tension or pain

Chest pain

Fatigue

Upset stomach

Sleep problems

Depression

I understand that the initial reaction at the onset of adversity is to panic and worry, but immediately you should remember the promises of God and gain strength from there. Pray and declare by faith that what you are going through is just a minor speed bump. Thank God in advance for victory because he has already made a way for you to escape the situation you are in. The next verse is the result of rejoicing, keeping calm, not worrying, praying and being thankful:

Philippians 4:7 - and the peace of God, which surpasses all understanding, will guard your hearts and minds through Christ Jesus.

You will have peace in the midst of the trial and

you won't even understand how. You will begin to realize that God is with you, He is on your side and nothing is too hard for Him. All of a sudden that problem isn't the center of attention anymore. Your attention has been shifted to the Word of God. Imagine yourself filling an empty container with food. Once the food reach the top of the container it becomes impossible for anything else to fit inside it. In the same way, you should be so full of joy and faith that fear, worry, and negativity has no room to get in.

Peace is guarding the door to your mind and your heart and nothing negative can get pass, unless you allow it. The circumstances that we find ourselves in should not dictate how we should feel. We are not victims of circumstance. We are not supposed to be like thermometers, changing with the temperature, but we should be more like thermostats and change our atmosphere. This is more than positive thinking. This is purposely setting your thoughts on the Word of God, remaining calm, rejoicing and staying this way no matter what is happening around you. Just as you would set a thermostat to a certain degree. In the book of John, Jesus, the Prince of Peace, tells us why we should use these keys of rejoicing, calmness, and thankfulness to unlock the door to peace:

John 16:33 [Amplified] - I have told you these

things, so that in Me you may have [perfect] peace and confidence. In the world you have tribulation and trials and distress and frustration; but be of good cheer [take courage; be confident, certain, undaunted]! For I have overcome the world. [I have deprived it of power to harm you and have conquered it for you.]

Random Declaration:

No matter what is happening in my life right now, I choose to believe God. I choose to trust God. I choose not to worry about anything because God has everything under control!

Praise God in Advance

2 Chronicles 20:17 – You will not need to fight in this battle. Position yourselves, stand still and see the salvation of the Lord, who is with you, O Judah and Jerusalem!

I have a question for you... What is your immediate response when adversity comes? Do you get angry? Do you try to put plans in place in order to fix it? Do you get scared and start worrying? What do you do? In 2 Chronicles 20 Jehoshaphat, King of Judah, has just received word that a great multitude is coming to battle against him. As King, I think, the immediate response to a coming war would be to stand strong and prepare the men for battle. However, his immediate response was fear. We all experience fear. Fear is a normal human response when something threatening, dangerous, or painful arises, but what is your response to fear? Do you worry? Let's see Jehoshaphat's response:

2 Chronicles 20:3-4 – And Jehoshaphat feared, and set himself to seek the Lord, and proclaimed a fast throughout all Judah. So Judah gathered together to ask help from the Lord...

The correct response is to go to God for help. As I said last week, God does not want us to handle things on our own. He wants us to seek him. Jehoshaphat did not try to put a plan in place to fix this situation on his own. He and the whole city went to God in prayer. More importantly, notice his prayer in verses 5-13. He reminds God of a promise he made to them and then confesses his total dependence on Him. This is why it is so important to know the promises of God in the scriptures. It's not that God needs to be reminded of what he said, after all he knows all and he does not have a bad memory; but think about this: When we go to God in prayer and repeat His promises, we are not really reminding God of them, but rather reminding ourselves, building our faith (confidence) in Him. After seeking the Lord in prayer, here is God's response:

2 Chronicles 20:15 – "Listen, all you of Judah, inhabitants of Jerusalem, and King Jehoshaphat! Thus says the Lord to you: 'Do not be afraid nor dismayed because of this great multitude, for the battle is not yours, but God's.

2 Chronicles 20:17 – "You will not need to fight in this battle. Position yourselves, stand still and see the salvation of the Lord, who is with you"

This is God's assurance of victory. God told them that this is a battle that they do not have to fight. The battle that you are in right now is not a battle that you are supposed to fight. That battle is the Lord's. Stop trying to fight! Stop trying to fix it! Stop worrying about it! Position yourself, stand still and see the salvation of the Lord! But wait, what does this mean 'position yourselves? Position yourself for what? Let's see….

2 Chronicles 20:22 – And when they began to sing and to praise, the Lord set ambushes against the people of Ammon, Moab, and Mount Seir, who had come against Judah; and they were defeated.

Position yourself means to get ready! Whether you see the battle forming or have found yourself in the midst of the battle, Get ready to praise God in advance for victory. The Word of the Lord is telling you right now: Do not be afraid, nor dismayed. This is a battle that you do not have to fight! This battle is the Lord's. Have you just received some bad news? Have you found yourself face to face with an overwhelming situation? Today, choose to follow the example of King Jehoshaphat and go to God in prayer, pray his promises, move your 'self' out of the way and confess your total dependence on Him. When you seek him, you will realize that he has already taken care of the problem for you. Stand still

and see the salvation of the Lord, who is with you!
Go ahead, praise him because the battle has been
won.

Jehovah Azar

Exodus 3:14-15 - And God said unto Moses, I Am That I Am: and he said, Thus shalt thou say unto the children of Israel, I Am hath sent me unto you. 15 And God said moreover unto Moses, Thus shalt thou say unto the children of Israel, the Lord God of your fathers, the God of Abraham, the God of Isaac, and the God of Jacob, hath sent me unto you: this is my name for ever, and this is my memorial unto all generations.

Here in Exodus, Moses is taking the sheep for a walk on the backside of the desert when he comes to the mountain of God and sees this bush on fire, but not burning. Moses is intrigued by this and says (paraphrasing): "This is amazing! I am going to get a little closer to this bush so I can see how this is happening!" So when God sees him getting closer to the bush He calls to Moses and tells him not to step any further until he takes off his shoes because the ground he is standing on is holy. Then God introduces himself to Moses as the God of Abraham, Isaac, and Jacob and then says:

Exodus 3:7 - And the Lord said, I have surely seen the affliction of my people which are in Egypt,

and have heard their cry by reason of their
taskmasters; for I know their sorrows;

Right at that moment when you think God is not
hearing you because you have prayed the same
prayer over and over, know that God has seen what
you are going through. He has heard your cry by
reason of your "taskmasters"; He knows your
sorrows and God has responded:

Exodus 3:8 - And I am come down to deliver
them out of the hand of the Egyptians, and to bring
them up out of that land unto a good land, unto a
land flowing with milk and honey; unto the place
of the Canaanites, and the Hittites, and the
Amorites, and the Perizzites, and the Hivites, and
the Jebusites.

I've heard people many times talk about the God
of the Old Testament being this angry and mean God.
This is not true. Look at what God did: He uses
Moses as a mouthpiece and literally comes in the
form of fire and a cloud to help them. This is a
loving God, more so a loving Father. Now to the
point: Moses asks (paraphrasing again): " Well, God
of Abraham, Isaac, and Jacob, I will do what you say,
but what should I tell them when they ask me your
name?" When we pray, our prayers seem to start like

this: "Lord, help me", "Lord, I need....", "God, I can't handle....", "Jesus, I don't know what to do about...." Take a moment to imagine the prayers of the Israelites: So many cries, so many needs are coming out of their mouths. When God tells Moses His name He says his name is "I AM" , "I AM THAT I AM". What does this mean? Look at this like a fill-in-the-blank statement: I AM _____. THAT, (what you just said), I AM. God is saying "I am everything they asked for and everything they will ask for. I am whatever they need and whatever they want." In the Old Testament what did the people need?

They needed help and He sent Moses & Aaron. They needed shade and he became a cloud to cover them during the day. They needed heat and he became a pillar of fire to keep them warm at night. They needed food and He gave them manna every morning. They wanted meat so he gave them quail. They needed water and He gave them water. They needed to cross a sea; He parted it so they could walk across on dry land. They asked for rules; he gave them the Commandments. They asked for a King; He gave them Saul. And so on....

In the New Testament what did the people need? They needed a savior; He sent Himself in His son, Jesus. They needed a renewed way of life and thinking; He sent Jesus with the good news of the Gospel. It needed to reach us and the entire world, so he sent the disciples. The people needed healing and He sent Jesus & the disciples to lay hands on them. The disciples needed power, so He sent the Holy Spirit. Peter needed money to pay taxes; He put money in a fish's mouth for him. In the midst of a storm , in fear, he gave them Peace. They needed Faith so He gave His Word. And so on...

God is our helper and has always been our helper. We talk about how wrong the Israelites were for not realizing God as their deliverer even after all He had done for them. But, today, are we any different??? Will the generations after you look at your life and say the same thing about you? Just like with the Israelites, He has shown us over and over and over again in the Bible and in our daily lives that He loves us and is with us to help us. Yet, we still doubt, we still complain, and we still worry just like the Israelites did. And Why? Truth be told, we are complaining, worrying, and doubting ourselves because we can't handle the mess we are in.

Find freedom in this: God never meant for us to handle anything on our own. Need Help? Hebrews 13:6a says: "So we can say with confidence, "The LORD is my helper, so I will have no fear." What do you need today? Jehovah Azar means God is our helper. Think about and meditate on this: There is no need to worry if you truly believe that God is there to help you. Stop trying to handle things on your own. Choose this day to stand firm in your belief that He is whatever you need and worry no more. At the end of Exodus 3:15, God says "This is my name for ever." I declare to you today that I AM THAT I AM has sent me to tell you that HE IS whatever you need.

Gardening 101

Genesis 8:22 - While the earth remains, seedtime and harvest, cold and heat, summer and winter, and day and night shall not cease

Let's talk about gardening. The basic principle of gardening is if you sow a seed you will reap a harvest. For example, if I plant a corn seed I will reap a harvest of corn. A lot of times when I hear people talking about "reaping what you sow" it's always about revenge or something negative. However, this law of seedtime and harvest (sowing and reaping) applies to everything in our lives.

Galatians 6:7 - Do not be deceived: God is not mocked, for whatever one sows, that will he also reap.

Proverbs 18:20 - A man's [moral] self shall be filled with the fruit of his mouth; and with the consequence of his words he must be satisfied [whether good or evil].

The words we speak are seeds, and whether positive or negative we will reap the consequences of things we say. What are you speaking? What are you saying about the circumstance you are in? Are you speaking the facts about your circumstances: "I'm sick", "I'm lonely", "I don't have the money to pay this bill!" If we ONLY speak the facts, we are accepting the circumstance. Instead, we should speak the truth about our circumstances. The fact may be that I have a bill due next week and I don't have the money to pay it, but the truth is my God shall supply all my need (Phil 4:19). God's Words (His promises) are seeds. If you think about a pack of seeds, it shows you on the package a picture of what that seed "promises" to harvest. Well, God's promises show you a picture of what you will receive as a harvest.

Let's look at the process of gardening using healing as an example:

1.   You want healing

2.   Get your pack of seeds (the bible) and find a seed that promises a harvest of healing: Isaiah 53:5

3.   You plant the seed by speaking it over the situation: ...'by Jesus' wounds I am healed'

4.   Boom! Harvest, right??........WRONG!

Remember it is SEED....TIME.... AND

HARVEST. When you plant a seed, its harvest doesn't spring up immediately. There is TIME. This is the place where I think most of us get frustrated, feel rejected, feel alone, start complaining and in a few cases give up. But think about the farmer who plants seeds. Does he plant a corn seed then get frustrated and complain because it didn't give him a harvest of corn right then, the next day, or the next week? No. He waters it, he pulls weeds, he sprinkle some miracle grow on it, and he waits having FAITH that the corn will grow. In fact, because he has so much FAITH in the picture he saw on the package, he EXPECTS TO SEE CORN AT HARVEST TIME.

A lot of us are in this waiting period right now. I want to encourage you to exercise your faith by seeing a picture of your need met, speak God's word in faith and EXPECT IT to happen! Thank God in advance for your harvest because you know its coming. Don't let the circumstance you are in make you forget about the seed you've planted. Don't destroy the seed you've planted by complaining or speaking negativity over it. Speak the truth about the circumstance because the truth of God's word ALWAYS nullify the facts of the circumstance. No matter what is happening around you, be strong in faith and have confidence that God, The Lord of the harvest (Matthew 9:38), will bring forth your harvest!

There is Power in Your Praise

Acts 16:25 - But about midnight, as Paul and Silas were praying and singing hymns of praise to God, and the [other] prisoners were listening to them,

Many people think that praising God is circumstantial. Some Christians only praise God when their circumstances are good and they have a reason to thank Him. What about when your circumstances are not so good? Here is an example of a situation that is not so good: Paul and his team are going from town to town spreading the gospel of Jesus. While in Philippi, Paul and Silas are accused of causing confusion in the city by encouraging practices that were "unlawful" and not observed by the Romans. The authorities right then and there strip Paul and Silas of their clothes, beat them in the middle of the street in front of everybody, haul them to prison, throw them in a dungeon and fasten their feet in stocks. Stocks are the wooden boards around the legs of the men in the picture. A person whose feet are in these things aren't going anywhere. This is a pretty bad situation.

Paul and Silas of course had the option of complaining or fighting, but they chose Option C (see last week's post) and started praising God. This seems like an unlikely response right, but I totally understand why they praised God. What else could they do? This situation is totally beyond their control. They can't move, crying and pleading wouldn't help, and fighting with the guards would have just made things worse for them. We must realize that when circumstances are too hard for us handle, or when situations are beyond our control, we need to just step back and praise God. Why? There is POWER in your praise. Anytime a negative circumstance comes, rejoice in the Lord. Philippians 4:4 tells us to Rejoice in the Lord always. Not only when times are good, but even when times are bad. Even when we don't feel like it, praise God anyway. In Psalms 103, it is clear that David is making himself praise God at a moment he didn't feel like it. Notice he is talking to himself:

Psalms 103:1-2 - Bless the Lord, O my soul: and all that is within me, bless his holy name.2 Bless the Lord, O my soul, and forget not all his benefits

Nehemiah 8:10 tells us that "The joy of the Lord is our strength" We receive strength from praise.

Let's look at what happened while Paul and Silas

were praising God:

Acts 16: 25-26 - But about midnight, as Paul and Silas were praying and singing hymns of praise to God, and the [other] prisoners were listening to them,26 Suddenly there was a great earthquake, so that the very foundations of the prison were shaken; and at once all the doors were opened and everyone's shackles were unfastened.

I love how the passage gives the exact moment when this happened: At midnight. Midnight is the transition time from one day to the next. I'm telling you that while you are praising God a transition takes place: the transition from breakdown to breakthrough. When you praise God it takes your focus off of yourself and your situation and places your attention on God. When you praise, God shows up and shake the foundations of that circumstance and loose you from it. But wait, not only did Paul's and Silas' praise loose them, but it loosed everyone around them that were bound. This is awesome because your praise can affect your surroundings, your whole family, and your friends. No matter what is happening in your life right now, realize that your praise has power in it. Praise God because God shows up when you praise. Stop complaining, stop fussing, stop trying to work and figure things out. Let go, praise God, and let God do the rest.

Option C

Daniel 3:17 - ... Our God whom we serve is able to deliver us from the burning fiery furnace, and He will deliver us from your hand, O king.

In Daniel chapter 3, King Nebuchadnezzar erected a golden image for the people to worship. The decree was that everyone had to fall down and worship this golden image when they heard the symphony play the worship music. If anyone decided not to worship he would be thrown into the middle of a burning fiery furnace. What extreme pressure to put on someone!

Option A. Bow and worship this golden image.

Option B. Die

That being said, when the people heard the music, they fell down to worship the golden image. Everybody was going with the flow of this program except three guys named Shadrach, Meshach, and Abed-Nego. When the king's counselors found them not following orders, they told the king. King Nebuchadnezzar, enraged, summons them and asks (paraphrasing): "I heard that you do not serve my gods or worship the golden image I set up. But if you hear the music at worship time and fall down and worship the golden image I set up, Good! If not, immediately I will throw you in the middle of the furnace. And who is the god who will deliver you from me?"

Challenge Accepted!

Shadrach, Meshach, and Abed-Nego told King Nebuchadnezzar (paraphrasing again) "Oh, Nebuchadnezzar, we do not have to entertain these statements you're making. But if it is the case that you need an answer: Our God whom we serve is able to deliver us from the burning fiery furnace, and He will deliver us from you, O King." Notice the faith of these guys. They had total confidence that God would save them from this situation. This is the faith that you and I should have all the time, no matter the situation. Ephesians 4:27 says "Do not allow the devil to get a foothold" This means don't entertain his ideas. Don't give him or his lies a second thought. Just like these guys, we should know our God and know what he will do for us. Romans 8:31 says "…If God be for us, who can be against us?"

Enraged King Nebuchadnezzar turned the heat up seven times hotter than normal, tied Shadrach,

Meshach, and Abed-Nego up and threw them and their belongings in the furnace. It was so hot in there that the men who threw them in died outside the furnace. Then something awesome happened:

Daniel 3:24-25 - Then King Nebuchadnezzar was astonished; and he rose in haste and spoke, saying to his counselors, "Did we not cast three men bound into the midst of the fire?" They answered and said to the king, "True, O king." "Look!" he answered, "I see four men loose, walking in the midst of the fire; and they are not hurt, and the form of the fourth is like the Son of God."

They tossed three bound (tied up) men in, but when the King looked closer, he saw four men in there walking around. The Lord came in, protected them and freed them of the ties that bound them. I'm telling you no matter how great the circumstance is, our God is greater and he is a deliverer! Just when the enemy thinks he has you, the Son of God shows up.

Daniel 3:27 - ...and they saw these men on whose bodies the fire had not power; the hair of their head was not singed nor were their garments affected, and the smell of fire was not on them.

When you totally rely and depend on God in the

midst of the fiery trial, you will come out on the other end unharmed and unscathed. Jesus is our savior. He not only saves our souls, but also saves us from anything we need saving from. When the enemy comes and turns the heat up it's easy to go with flow of the circumstance and complain. Things may even feel out your control and you are right. Realize that things are out of your control because God has everything under control. When adversity comes and presents your options of A & B: give in or be consumed, choose Option C: Confidence in God. He will show up and show off his miraculous power in your life. He will never ever let you down.

Random Declaration:

Just as God was with Shadrach, Meshach, and Abed-Nego, I know that when I am going through a difficut time, God is with me in middle of it. I know God is helping me through this and I will be unscathed.

The Faith Test

John 6:5-6 - Jesus looked up then, and seeing that a vast multitude was coming toward Him, He said to Philip, Where are we to buy bread, so that all these people may eat? 6 But He said this to prove (test) him, for He well knew what He was about to do.

Here in this passage of John 6, Jesus and his disciples have sat down to rest on a mountainside. Jesus looks up and see that a great multitude is coming toward him. Seeing this he leans over to Philip and asks him a question even though He already knew what He was going to do for the people. The question is:

John 6:5 - ... Where are we to buy bread, so that all these people may eat?

Even though Jesus is the one asking this question, it is a test to gauge the faith of his disciples. This type of question is so familiar. When a "great circumstance" approach you, similar questions arise: "How am I going to handle this situation?" "Where am I going to get the money pay this?" "This is too 'great' to handle, what am I going to do?!" In that moment, just as Jesus was testing his disciples, your faith is being tested and your response matters. Let's look at the response of two of his disciples:

John 6:7 - Philip answered Him, Two hundred pennies' (forty dollars) worth of bread is not enough that everyone may receive even a little.

Philip's response to this question is one most of us would say. "I don't have enough money." His immediate response was to worry about money. He, like most, is looking at their own available resources only. Philip have seen Jesus do miracles, yet it didn't cross his mind that he could do one right then. When a great circumstance come, you look at your money, you look at your friends/family for help, you try everything in your power, then finally you think of Jesus. This is the wrong response.

John 6:8-9 - Another of His disciples, Andrew, Simon Peter's brother, said to Him, 9 There is a little boy here, who has [with him] five barley loaves, and two small fish; but what are they among so many people?

Andrew is showing his lack of faith by looking a the circumstances, looking at the resources, and limiting God's ability to use them. He tells Jesus, that it is impossible to feed so many with 2 fish and 5 barley loaves. This is the wrong response. Do not limit God's abilities. **Here is the Faith Test!** This is a great, overwhelming situation! What am I going to do?

a) Look at the situation, look at what I have available and Worry because it's not enough

b) Do everything in my own ability and power

c) Limit God ability to help

d) Recline (Relax)

The correct response is......

John 6:10 - Jesus said, Make all the people recline....

At the moment when your faith is tested, choose to recline (or relax) remembering that God has everything under control. Matthew 6:8 says ..."for your Father knows what you need before you ask Him." The Lord is compassionate and He already knows about your situation. He has already provided for you. Jesus was in control of this circumstance with a great multitude and took a 2pc. fish dinner and multiplied it to feed them and had some bread left over. I urge you, do not focus on your available resources only. Put your focus on the one who can not only meet your need, but exceed your needs and expectations! Do you truly believe that God is able to meet your need no matter how "great" it is? Jeremiah 32:27 says "Behold, I am the Lord, the God of all flesh; is there anything too hard for Me?" Nothing is too hard for our God, so relax!

What's that in your hand?

Exodus 4:2 - And the Lord said to him, What is that in your hand? And he said, A rod.

Moses has just been chosen by God to deliver His people out of Pharaoh hands. Even though God promises to be with Moses the whole way, he gives every excuse to get out of doing what God wants him to do: He doesn't feel deserving, he doesn't know God's name, he feels the people will not believe him, and he feels he isn't good with words. Moses is thinking of every reason why what God is saying won't work. When you are going through a tough time, Have you thought of excuses for why your needs aren't met or why miracles aren't happening in your life? "Well I havent' prayed in a while..." or "I just messed up last night, or "This circumstance is just too great ...." You've thought of every reason for why what God has promised to you is not working in your life. You, just like Moses, are looking at the circumstances. God responds to Moses' excuses with a simple yet profound question:

Exodus 4:2 - And the Lord said to him, What is that in your hand? And he said, A rod.

Let's look at this rod:

It was used to confront the Egyptian soothsayers – Exodus 7:12.

It was used to turn the waters of Egypt to blood – Exodus 7:17-20.

It was used to bring forth the plague of frogs – Exodus 8:5.

It was used to bring forth the plague of lice – Exodus 8:16.

It was used to bring forth the plague of thunder and hail – Exodus 9:23.

It was used to call and east wind that blew in the plague of locusts – Exodus 10:13.

It was used to part the Red Sea – Exodus 14:16.

It was used to cause the Red Sea to come together again, drowning Pharaoh and his army – Exodus 14:27.

It was used to bring water from a rock in the desert – Exodus 17:5.

It was used to bring victory over the Amalekites – Exodus 17:9.

This was not just a rod. When God asked Moses what was in his hand He was not asking this question for information, He was bringing something to Moses' attention and this is the point that God want to make to us this week: God is saying stop making excuses, stop looking at the circumstances, look at what's in your hand. Look at what you possess. God is saying Everything you need to have miracles manifested in your life, is in your hands. Don't worry about what you've done wrong, God has still equipped you with power to overcome any obstacle.

Remember Moses murdered someone and God still gave him power to overcome the obstacles in the way. God has given you power through speaking His word and standing firm in faith in His word. This is the "rod" that is currently in your hands! You know what that rod represented? It represented potential. Every word you speak has the potential to become your reality. Just like that simple rod became so much more. I encourage you today, to stop looking around at the circumstances, stop makin excuses, stop complaining, and start using what's in your hand.

Are you frustrating a miracle?

John 11:35 – Jesus wept.

John 11 is the account where Lazarus is raised from the dead. The passage begins with Jesus receiving word that Lazarus is sick. He then tells His disciples that they are going back to Bethany to "wake up" Lazarus. The disciples are complaining that the Jews there want to kill Him and it makes no sense to go back, and if Lazarus is just sleeping, he will be alright. Jesus senses the unbelief in them and says:

John 11:14-16 - So then Jesus told them plainly, Lazarus is dead, 15 And for your sake I am glad that I was not there; it will help you to believe (to trust and rely on Me). However, let us go to him.

Jesus is now making His way back to Bethany to raise Lazarus from the dead and on the way He runs into Martha who lets Him know that if He had been there her brother would not have died, but she knows that whatever He ask of God, God would give it to Him. Seeing her burst of faith, Jesus tells her "Your brother will rise again". "I know he will, in the resurrection in the Last Day" Martha says. But Jesus responds:

John 11:25-26 - Jesus said to her, I am [Myself] the Resurrection and the Life. Whoever believes in (adheres to, trusts in, and relies on) Me, although he may die, yet he shall live; 26 And whoever continues to live and believes in (has faith in, cleaves to, and relies on) Me shall never [actually] die at all. Do you believe this?

Jesus is telling the reason He is going to the cross. Jesus is saying that He is the means by which we will be put back in "right standing" (with God) and able to live an abundant life. Verse 25 - Resurrection and Life in the Greek text are "anastasis" meaning "standing up right" and "dzo-ay" meaning "abundant life." Jesus says this plainly in John 10.

John 10:10 - ... I came that they may have and enjoy life, and have it in abundance (to the full, till it overflows).

As Jesus proceeds, He runs into Mary.

John 11:32-33 - When Mary came to the place where Jesus was and saw Him, she dropped down at His feet, saying to Him, Lord, if You had been here, my brother would not have died. When Jesus saw her sobbing, and the Jews who came with her [also] sobbing, He was deeply moved in spirit and troubled. [He chafed in spirit and sighed and was disturbed.]

Jesus asks where is Lazarus and then....

John 11:35-38 Jesus wept.36 The Jews said, See how He loved him! 37 But some of them said, Could not He Who opened a blind man's eyes have prevented this man from dying? 38 Now Jesus, again sighing repeatedly and deeply disquieted, approached the tomb.

I believe Jesus wept at the state everyone was in. He was surrounded by unbelief. Jesus was not moved with compassion. He was uneasy and frustrated. Jesus is trying to make His way to Lazarus to do a miracle, but He is being stopped along the way. Question: Is your level of faith frustrating a miracle from taking place in your life?

Let's look at these levels of faith described in this chapter: The disciples represent those who have experienced the goodness & grace of God in their lives and still stumble in faith. (ref John 11:9-10 - Jesus answered, Are there not twelve hours in the day? Anyone who walks about in the daytime does not stumble, because he sees [by] the light of this world. 10 But if anyone walks about in the night, he does stumble, because there is no light in him [the light is lacking to him]. Here Jesus is referencing John 8:12 - *"Once more Jesus addressed the crowd. He said, I am the Light of the world. He who follows Me will not be walking in the dark, but will have the Light which is Life". (The 12 hours in the day represent His 12 disciples who had seen Him do miracles and still stumbled in their confidence in Him))*.

Martha represents those with the quick burst of faith (confidence) during the preaching of the Word, then forget about it when adversity comes. She told Jesus she believed Him when He said her brother would rise again, but then when Jesus tells them to roll the stone away she forgets that Jesus told her this. (ref John 11:39-40) Mary represents those who limit God and surround themselves with the wrong people and end up having a pity party. They surround themselves with people who have little or no faith at all. Mary knows Jesus can heal the sick, but didn't even think that He could exceed their expectations. *(ref John 11:32)*

Regardless of the unbelief around him Jesus still called to Lazarus, and he who was dead four days walked out of the tomb. A passage that is normally read as Jesus just doing another miracle turns out to be about so much more. Jesus loves you and he wants you to have an enjoyable, full, worry-free life. The Lord wants us to totally trust and believe in Him. Don't allow unbelief to frustrate the blessings that God wants to get to you. Remember that Jesus is there to help you. Stay strong in faith and the seemingly dead, or hopeless situations in your life will be brought back to life.

Stand Firm! Be strong in your faith!

Matthew 6:25-26 - Therefore I tell you, stop being perpetually uneasy (anxious and worried) about your life,... Look at the birds of the air; they neither sow nor reap nor gather into barns, and yet your heavenly Father keeps feeding them. Are you not worth much more than they?

Worrying means to feel uneasy or concerned about something; to be troubled. Matthew has told us here: there is nothing to worry about. He also gives us a great example using birds. Birds don't plant seeds, reap a harvest, and store up food for later. God supplies them with food when they need it. Aren't we, his children, worth more than they? He doesn't want us to worry about anything that is happening in our lives right now or ever. Do we gain anything positive by worrying about a problem? Will worrying about that problem change that problem? Matthew asks:

Matthew 6:27 - Can any one of you by worrying add a single hour to your life?

No Matt, we can't and this is why we shouldn't worry. Worrying causes anxiety which then leads to physical illnesses. Peter gives some great advice about what to do with the things that cause us to worry:

1Peter 5:7 - "Casting the whole of your care [all your anxieties, all your worries, all your concerns, once and for all] on Him, for He cares for you affectionately and cares about you watchfully. "

When you pray and give that problem over to the Lord, LET HIM KEEP IT. When you worry about it later, you take that problem back and put it on your shoulders to carry. Consider this: worrying implies that you do not totally trust God and/or you do not completely believe God's Word concerning your situation. We have to throw our worries on Him and…

1Peter 5:8 - Be sober, be vigilant; because your adversary the devil, as a roaring lion, walks about, seeking whom he may devour:

Peter is telling us to be alert and aware of this tactic of the devil. He walks around as a roaring lion. When a lion roars it's to scare and intimidate the prey. The devil has been around for a looooong time and he knows people (humans) and what will intimidate us and make us worry. He will try anything. The key word in this verse is "MAY". This word "may" imply that he "may" or "may not" consume you. He could possibly pass on by. Let's see what would make him do this...

1Peter 5:9 - Withstand him; be firm in faith [against his onset—rooted, established, strong, immovable, and determined],...

Standing firm in faith (your confidence in God) will show him he can't get under your skin. The devil may let out a loud roar, but you can roar a louder one right back at him with a promise from God's Word in it and he will know he has to pass on by. The bible says in James 4:7 - ...Resist the devil, and he will flee from you. This means to ignore him! Worrying acknowledges that the devil has gotten to you. Don't give him that credit. You may be going through a trying circumstance right now, and you don't have to deny your circumstance, but you can deny the circumstance the right to consume you. Choose to believe what the Word of God says about your circumstance and instead of saying "I don't know how...", or "I'm worried about..." Stand strong in faith and choose to say: "I TRUST GOD." Anytime you feel yourself starting to worry about something remember this promise from Jesus:

John 16:33 - I have told you these things, so that in Me you may have [perfect] peace and confidence. In the world you have tribulation and trials and distress and frustration; but be of good cheer [take courage; be confident, certain, undaunted]! For I have overcome the world. [I have deprived it of power to harm you and have conquered it for you.]

Random Declaration:

I do not worry about anything. I know that I am protected. Because I am in the secret place of the Most High, I am safe from all hurt, harm, and danger

Underneath his Wings

Today we are living in really hard times. Every time you turn on the news or radio there is always a depressing story being told. There is the issue with Russia and Ukraine, victims of bullying have begun to resort to suicide, violence is at an all time high... the list could go on & on. If it's not one thing, it's another. Moreover it is sad to say that in this world wrong is viewed as right, and right is viewed as wrong. I think even the Earth is groaning at all that is going on; notice the changes in the weather. In the midst of all that's happening, where can we find peace? This week, the Lord is telling us to meditate on this passage. Take your time, read it carefully and let it minister to you:

Psalms 91

1 He who dwells (stays) in the secret place of the Most High shall remain stable and fixed under the shadow (shelter or shade) of the Almighty [Whose power no foe can withstand].

2 I will say of the Lord, He is my Refuge and my Fortress, my God; on Him I lean and rely, and in Him I [confidently] trust!

3 For [then] He will deliver you from the snare of the fowler (bird catcher) and from the deadly pestilence (disease).

4 [Then] He will cover you with His pinions (the outer part of a bird's wing including the flight feathers.), and under His wings shall you trust and find refuge; His truth and His faithfulness are a shield and a buckler.

5 You shall not be afraid of the terror of the night, nor of the arrow (the evil plots and slanders of the wicked) that flies by day,

6 Nor of the pestilence that stalks in darkness, nor of the destruction and sudden death that surprise and lay waste at noonday.

7 A thousand may fall at your side, and ten thousand at your right hand, but it shall not come near you.

8 Only a spectator shall you be [yourself inaccessible in the secret place of the Most High] as you witness the reward of the wicked.

9 Because you have made the Lord your refuge,

and the Most High your dwelling place,

10 There shall no evil befall you, nor any plague or calamity come near your tent (home).

11 For He will give His angels [especial] charge over you to accompany and defend and preserve you in all your ways [of obedience and service].

12 They shall bear you up on their hands, lest you dash your foot against a stone.(in case you stumble or trip)

13 You shall tread upon the lion and adder; the young lion and the serpent shall you trample underfoot.

Then God says this about each of us:

14 Because he has set his love upon Me, therefore will I deliver him; I will set him on high, because he knows and understands My name [has a personal knowledge of My mercy, love, and kindness—trusts and relies on Me, knowing I will never forsake him, no, never].

15 He shall call upon Me, and I will answer him; I will be with him in trouble, I will deliver him and honor him.

16 With long life will I satisfy him and show him My salvation.

When you are watching the news, listening to the radio, or when that issue that is going on in your personal life start to weigh you down, remember this Psalm. Know He will let nothing overwhelm or harm you or your loved ones. I want to encourage you to keep your focus on God. Keep your faith and confidence in Him at a high level. The Lord is with you to help you & protect you. Remain under the wings of the Almighty God.

Expectation

Matthew 9:29 - Then touched He their eyes, saying, According to your faith be it unto you.

Here in Matthew 9, Jesus has left Jairus' home headed to another destination. Meanwhile, following Him are two blind men yelling for Him to have mercy on them and heal them. Close your eyes and imagine walking out of your home (with your hands stretched out), into a throng of people, not sure if the person you are looking for is behind you or in front of you. You feel your way through these people, hoping to find who you are looking for. You hear everyone around you yelling to this guy named Jesus, who you heard could open blinded eyes. You began to yell to him too because he must be near and you hope He hears your yelling over the other yells. This was the circumstance of the two blind men this day. What made them go through all this?

In that same throng of people, the woman with the issue of blood, who heard that anyone that touched Jesus became well, is pressing her way to Him too. What made this hemorrhaging woman leave her home, go into the streets, despite her circumstances, just like these blind men, determined to find Jesus. What they heard about Jesus made them determined to find Him, but most importantly, when they found Him they expected to be healed. Let's talk about Expectation.

Expectation is a strong belief that something will happen. (emphasis on will) The blind men finally reached Jesus:

Matthew 9:28-30 - When he entered the house, the blind men came to him, and Jesus said to them, "Do you believe that I am able to do this?" They said to him, "Yes, Lord." Then he touched their eyes, saying, "According to your faith be it done to you." 30 And their eyes were opened.

Jesus asked if they believed, then He tested their expectation by telling them "according to your faith, be it unto you". Faith and expectation go hand in hand. You cannot have one without the other if you want to see a miracle manifested in your life. Expectation is the birthplace of miracles. Most times you don't get what you desire, you get what you expect. Remember Acts chapter 3, there was a crippled man asking for alms as people went into the temple. When the crippled man saw Peter and John he asked them for a gift. Peter directed the crippled man to look at him and John and the bible says:

Acts 3:5 - And [the man] paid attention to them, expecting that he was going to get something from them.

Peter told Him "I do not have any money, but what I do have, I will give it to you. In Jesus name, walk!" Peter took hold of the man's hand and the man immediately felt strength in his ankle bones and was able to walk and leap for joy. Expectation brings manifestation. The crippled man expected something, and he received healing. The blind men expected to see and they did, the hemorrhaging woman expected to be healed and she was. What do you need today? Do you believe Jesus is able to meet that need? If yes, Do not allow the things that go on around you influence your attitude, make you complain or make you lose hope. Remain constant & fixed on the confession of your faith that God has already met that need, and Expect to see the manifestation.

Determination

Mark 5:27-28 - She had heard the reports concerning Jesus, and she came up behind Him in the throng and touched His garment, 28 For she kept saying, If I only touch His garments, I shall be restored to health.

Jairus has just pleaded with Jesus to come to his home to lay hands on & heal his daughter, who is at the point of death. Jesus goes with Jairus and while they are walking a great crowd is following Him and pressing him from all sides so as almost to smother Him. In the midst of this crowd there is someone with a unique situation pressing their way, determined to get to Jesus:

Mark 5:25-26 - And there was a woman who had had a flow of blood for twelve years, 26 And who had endured much suffering under [the hands of] many physicians and had spent all that she had, and was no better but instead grew worse.

This woman could have stayed home and remained depressed and discouraged. She was considered unclean and anything she touched became unclean. Yet, she was looking for Jesus to touch him. Let's look at how a weak and hemorrhaging woman could press her way through a crowd:

Mark 5:27-28 - She had heard the reports concerning Jesus, and she came up behind Him in the throng and touched His garment, 28 For she kept saying, If I only touch His garments, I shall be restored to health.

The woman said her faith declaration of "If I only touch his garment, I shall be restored to health" over and over again. She was using her faith (her confidence in God) by "saying". Romans 10:9b says "and with the mouth he confesses (declares openly and speaks out freely his faith) and confirms [his] salvation (deliverance)." True faith is believing and confessing what God has already done by grace through Jesus and His finished work on the cross. Believe that it is already done. However, in this woman's case, Jesus hadn't gone to the cross yet, but she HEARD this:

Mark 3:10 - For he had healed many; insomuch that they pressed upon him for to touch him, as many as had plagues

She BELIEVED one thing: if she touched Jesus she would be whole. She believed it so much so that she could see herself healed. She saw it already done in her mind. So out the door she goes!

Faith does not move God, faith moves us. This woman's faith moved her out of her house, into the street to press her way through a throng, and despite the prevailing circumstances caused her to stretch out her hand to touch Jesus' garment. This woman was FOCUSED & DETERMINED. She found him and kept her eyes on him until she got closer and closer, until she touched him and when she did:

Mark 5:29 - And immediately her flow of blood was dried up at the source, and [suddenly] she felt in her body that she was healed of her [distressing] ailment.

Jesus stops in his tracks and looking around asks: "Who touched my clothes?" Keep in mind that there are many people touching Jesus in this crowd. However, there was something special about this woman's touch. It was a touch of faith and that touch of faith made her whole.

Mark 5:34 - And He said to her, Daughter, your faith (your trust and confidence in Me, springing from faith in God) has restored you to health. Go in (into) peace and be continually healed and freed from your [distressing bodily] disease.

This woman shows us not only the importance of faith, but also the reward that is yours when you exercise diligence and determination with your faith.

Be like this woman. She didn't let what was ailing
her stop her, she didn't let the crowd stop her, she
didn't let the purity laws stop her, she didn't let
anything stop her from getting the healing she
KNEW was hers if she touched Jesus. Do not allow
the circumstance you're in get you down and keep
you down. Even when you have suffered for a long
time, tried everything, ran out of money, and things
have gone from bad to worse, your belief that Jesus
has made a way for you, provided for you, or healed
you must dismiss the thought that your situation is
hopeless. With Jesus there is ALWAYS hope. Keep
pressing for your breakthrough.

Words

Job 22:28 (NKJV) - You will also declare a thing, And it will be established for you; So light will shine on your ways.

Remember that old saying "Sticks and stones may break my bones, but words will never hurt me?" I haven't heard this saying since I was a kid and that was some time ago. Kids used to say this when someone would call them names or say something bad about them. I've said it before and I bet many of you have also. The Lord brought this saying back to my memory because I was thinking about the power of words; more importantly the power of our words.

Genesis 1:26a says 'Then God said, "Let Us make man in Our image, according to Our likeness..."'

We are made in God's image and likeness which means we are like Him and we have the ability to do things the way He does things. Hebrews 11:3 says: *"By faith we understand that the* **worlds were framed by the word of God***, so that the things which are seen were not made of things which are visible."* God created the worlds with His words and we, being made in his image and likeness, are also able to create our "world" with our words. In this case "world" can be your environment, your body, mind, spirit, soul, or any situation you may be facing. Our words have the power to create change.

Proverbs 18:20-21 (MSG) - Words satisfy the mind as much as fruit does the stomach; good talk is as gratifying as a good harvest. Words kill, words give life; they're either poison or fruit—you choose.

You can change the situation you are in by changing the words you say. Changing the situation negatively or positively is up to you. So, sticks and stones may break your bones, but words **CAN** hurt you. Let's see what James has said on this subject:

James 3:3-5 (MSG) - A bit in the mouth of a horse controls the whole horse. A small rudder on a huge ship in the hands of a skilled captain sets a course in the face of the strongest winds. A word out of your mouth may seem of no account, but it can accomplish nearly anything—or destroy it!

James likens our tongue to bits in the horses' mouth that controls the horse and the rudder of a huge ship that sets the course of the ship. In the same way our tongue sets the direction of our lives down a good path or a bad path. The choice is ours.

So how do we set the course of our lives? Let's take a look at what Jesus did:

Luke 4:16-20 - So He came to Nazareth, where He had been brought up. And as His custom was, He went into the synagogue on the Sabbath day, and stood up to read. 17 And He was handed the book of the prophet Isaiah. And when He had opened the book, He found the place where it was written:

18 "The Spirit of the Lord is upon Me,
Because He has anointed Me
To preach the gospel to the poor;
He has sent Me to heal the brokenhearted,
To proclaim liberty to the captives
And recovery of sight to the blind,
To set at liberty those who are oppressed;
19 To proclaim the acceptable year of the Lord."

*20 Then He closed the book, and gave it back to the attendant and sat down. And the eyes of all who were in the synagogue were fixed on Him. 21 And He began to say to them, "Today this Scripture is fulfilled in your **hearing**."*

This is what Jesus did: He opens the book of Isaiah and **finds a scripture that applied to Him and read it out loud**. Jesus is our perfect example and this is what we are supposed to do. Earlier in this same chapter, Luke 4:1-13, Jesus uses the word of God to overcome the devil's tempting. Every time the devil tempted Him, he repeated the word of God. In both of these cases, Jesus used scriptures that applied to Him or the current situation and spoke it out loud. This is the key to creating change. God wants us to find out what His Word has to say about us or our situations and speak it to create a great outcome.

The words we speak can make or break us. If you need strength, speak strength into your life by finding scriptures on strength and repeating them. If its healing you need, find out what God's Word says about healing and say it. The key is speaking the Word out loud.

Revelations 12:11- And they overcame him by the blood of the Lamb and by the word of their testimony,...

We overcome the devil and his tactics because of Jesus and His finished work on the cross and by the **word of our testimony.** A testimony is a **spoken statement**, especially in a court of law. Just think you could be one word away from your breakthrough. If you will change your words, you will change your life.

Take that Step!

Matthew 14:28-29 - And Peter answered Him, Lord, if it is You, command me to come to You on the water. 29 He said, Come! So Peter got out of the boat and walked on the water, and he came toward Jesus.

I posted an entry ("Never Alone") from this same passage of scripture, but this time I am going to talk about it a bit differently. Jesus has just fed 5,000+ people and now He is directing the disciples to go ahead of Him to the other side while He dismisses the crowd. After he dismisses the crowd he goes into the hills to pray. Meanwhile, the disciples have encountered a terrible wind storm.

Matthew 12:24 - But the boat was by this time out on the sea, many furlongs [a furlong is one-eighth of a mile] distant from the land, beaten and tossed by the waves, for the wind was against them.

On top of that, in the middle of the night they notice something coming toward them:

Matthew 14:25-26 - And in the fourth watch [between 3:00—6:00 a.m.] of the night, Jesus came to them, walking on the sea. 26 And when the disciples saw Him walking on the sea, they were terrified and said, It is a ghost! And they screamed out with fright.

They are going through this storm, then they think they see a ghost approaching them. We all have been here. While in the midst of a storm of life, something you fear is approaching. If it's not one thing, it's another! At this point, the disciples are freaking out and so do we when we are in this type of circumstance! Jesus immediately says to them:

Matthew 14:27 - But instantly He spoke to them, saying, Take courage! I Am! Stop being afraid!

I've told you before in a previous post what "I AM" means (see post *12/10/13 - Jehovah Azar*). Jesus is saying, No matter how hard the winds are blowing, or how high the waves, I AM is here!!! Do not be afraid!

Matthew 14:28 - And Peter answered Him, Lord, if it is You, command me to come to You on the water.

What powerful words from Jesus, but still Peter needed proof. How many times have you heard a word from the Lord, and still didn't believe it?

Something very important happens next, Look:

Matthew 14:29 - He said, Come! So Peter got out of the boat and walked on the water, and he came toward Jesus.

This is how you get the proof: After you hear the Word, your next move is to take that step of faith out on what you just heard. Do you believe the Word or not? The bible says in James,

James 2:14 - What does it profit, my brethren, if someone says he has faith but does not have works?

James 2:26 - For as the body without the spirit is dead, so faith without works is dead also

Let's rephrase that this way: **What good is it, if someone says they believe something but does not act on it? For as the body without the spirit is dead, so believing without action is dead.**

Believing is an action. You can say you believe something but it means nothing until you act on it. For example, Peter **stepped** out of the boat. The boy **gave** his two fish and five loaves. (Matt 14:17-21)

The woman **reached** her hand out to touch Jesus' clothes.(Mark 5:27-29) The leper **stretched** out his hand. (Matt 12:13) All of the words in bold are action words. When these people acted on what they believed, a miracle happened. Mark 9:23 says "*all things are possible to him who believes!*"

What are you believeing God for today? Always remember if you don't take that step, you will remain in the same place. Take that step and act on what you believe. Do not be afraid. Your miracle is one "step" away.

The Treasure

2 Corinthians 4:7 - But we have this treasure in jars of clay, to show that the surpassing power belongs to God and not to us

Here in this passage Paul is giving an encouraging word regarding hardships. Paul knows a thing or two about hard times. He was persecuted, shipwrecked, beaten, imprisoned, etc. All of us experience hardships at some point in our lives. Maybe we have never been shipwrecked like Paul, but sometimes circumstances we go through can make our lives feel shipwrecked. It can be overwhelming at times, but one thing you should ALWAYS remember during the hardest of times: God has never and will never ever leave us. Friends and family may forsake us, but God will never leave us, forsake us, or fail us! No matter what we go through we have God, who created all things, knows all things, and is in control of all things on our side.

Paul is encouraging us by saying:

2 Corinthians 4:8-9 - We are afflicted in every way, but not crushed; perplexed, but not driven to despair; persecuted, but not forsaken; struck down, but not destroyed;

This treasure that we have is RESILIENCE.

Resilience means:

1. **the ability to spring back into shape; elasticity.**
2. **the capacity to recover quickly from difficulties; toughness.**

We may get knocked down, but we are not knocked out. It is by the power of God that we are able to get back up when afflictions rise up against us. Even the most terrible thing that can happen will only be a temporary delay. Paul continues to say:

2 Corinthians 4:16 - So we do not lose heart....

There are always going to be tough times, but never give up. Do not let the circumstance consume you. That circumstance you are experiencing may bruise you, but it can not break you. No matter what is happening in your life right now, trust in the power of God and BOUNCE BACK!

Declare:

When I am going through a difficult time, I know that God is with me and has made a way out for me. Hard times will come as part of life, but I am resilient. I have the ability to recover quickly. Nothing can keep me down! I am always victorious!

Have you made Jesus the Lord and Savior of your life?

Start your new life in Christ today!

Romans 10:1 - my heart's desire and prayer to God for them is that they may be saved.

Romans 10:9 - If you confess with your mouth that Jesus is Lord and believe in your heart that God raised him from the dead, you will be saved.

Romans 10:13 - For everyone who calls on the name of the Lord will be saved.

If you want to accept Jesus into your life, please say this prayer:

Jesus, I come to you confessing that I believe that You died for me and I repent of my sin. I ask you to come into my life. I believe with my heart and confess with my mouth that you, Jesus, are Lord and that you rose from the dead. I am now saved! Thank you Jesus for forgiving me, for saving me, and for loving me. Amen.

If you prayed this prayer to receive Jesus Christ as your Savior for the first time, please contact us on the web at **www.encouragingfaith.weebly.com** or email: **encouragingfaithblog@gmail.com**